JB LEWIS
McAneney, Caitie, author.
John Lewis : American
politician and civil rights
icon

BREAKOUT BIOGRAPHIES

JOHN LEWIS

American Politician and Civil Rights Icon

Caitie McAneney

PowerKiDS
press

Published in 2018 by The Rosen Publishing Group, Inc.
29 East 21st Street, New York, NY 10010

First Edition

Editor: Elizabeth Krajnik
Book Design: Tanya Dellaccio

Photo Credits: Cover Teresa Kroeger/WireImage/Getty Images; pp. 5 (top),13, 21 (bottom), 23
Bettmann/Getty Images; p. 5 (bottom) Rick Diamond/Getty Images Entertainment/Getty Images;
p. 7 (top) Joseph Sohm/Shutterstock.com; p. 7 (bottom) https://commons.wikimedia.org/wiki/
File:Greene_Co_Ga1941_Delano.jpg; p. 9 Historical/Corbis Historical/Getty Images; p. 11 (top) PAUL J.
RICHARDS/AFP/Getty Images; p. 11 (bottom) AFP/Getty Images; p. 15 (top) https://commons.wikimedia.
org/wiki/File:Rosa_Parks_being_fingerprinted_by_Deputy_Sheriff_D.H._Lackey_after_being_arrested_for_
boycotting_public_transportation_-_Original.jpg; p. 15 (bottom) Paul Schutzer/The LIFE Picture Collection/
Getty Images; p. 17 Robert Elfstrom/Villon Films/Archive Photos/Getty Images; p. 19 (top) Hulton Archive/
Getty Images; p. 19 (bottom) AFP/Getty Images; p. 21 (top) National Archives/Hulton Archive/Getty
Images; p. 25 (top) Alex Wong/Getty Images News/Getty Images; p. 25 (bottom) Ververidis Vasilis/
Shutterstock.com; p. 27 Allison Shelley/Getty Images News/Getty Images; p. 29 (top) SAUL LOEB/AFP/
Getty Images; p. 29 (bottom) Larry French/Getty Images Entertainment/Getty Images.

Library of Congress Cataloging-in-Publication Data

Names: McAneney, Caitie, author.
Title: John Lewis : American politician and civil rights icon / Caitie
  McAneney.
Description: New York : PowerKids Press, [2018] | Series: Breakout
  biographies | Includes index.
Identifiers: LCCN 2017027528| ISBN 9781538325490 (library bound) | ISBN
  9781538326190 (pbk.) | ISBN 9781538326206 (6 pack)
Subjects: LCSH: Lewis, John, 1940 February 21–Juvenile literature. |
  African American civil rights workers–Biography–Juvenile literature. |
  Civil rights workers–United States–Biography–Juvenile literature. |
  African American legislators–Biography–Juvenile literature. |
  Legislators–United States–Biography–Juvenile literature. | African
  Americans–Civil rights–History–20th century–Juvenile literature. |
  Civil rights movements–Southern States–History–20th century–Juvenile
  literature.
Classification: LCC E840.8.L43 M35 2018 | DDC 328.73/092 [B] –dc23
LC record available at https://lccn.loc.gov/2017027528

Manufactured in the United States of America

CPSIA Compliance Information: Batch #BW18PK For Further Information contact Rosen Publishing, New York, New York at 1-800-237-9932

CONTENTS

CIVIL RIGHTS ICON

John Lewis is one of the most important civil rights **icons** living today. By his early 20s, he was already one of the "Big Six" leaders of the American civil rights movement.

The American civil rights movement was a fight for basic freedoms and rights led primarily by African Americans. The modern movement happened mostly during the 1950s and 1960s, but people today are still fighting for equal rights for all.

Lewis was part of the original movement, and he's still part of the fight. He's been arrested, beaten, and treated unfairly, but he still believes in the promise of equality and justice for all Americans. Today, Lewis serves as a U.S. representative from Georgia. He uses his voice in the House of Representatives to speak up for Americans everywhere.

THE "BIG SIX"

Lewis, far left, was one of the "Big Six," a group of six representatives of civil right organizations during the 1960s. Lewis was chairman of the Student Nonviolent Coordinating Committee (SNCC) in 1963, when this photo was taken.

Others were, from left after Lewis, Whitney Young Jr. of the National Urban League (NUL); A. Philip Randolph of the Negro American Labor Council (NALC); Martin Luther King Jr. of the Southern Christian Leadership Conference (SCLC); James L. Farmer Jr. of the Congress of Racial Equality (CORE); and Roy Wilkins of the National Association for the Advancement of Colored People (NAACP).

John Lewis stands next to his arrest photographs from 1963, when he led nonviolent protests as part of the civil rights movement.

SON OF
SHARECROPPERS

John Lewis was born February 21, 1940, just outside of Troy, Alabama. His parents were sharecroppers. Sharecroppers lived on land owned by a landlord. The tenants worked the land in exchange for some of the crop. The other share of the crop went to the landlord as payment. This system often resulted in the sharecroppers owing the landlord more money. Some Americans considered sharecropping another form of slavery, but for many poor southerners, there was no other option.

Lewis grew up on a farm and went to **segregated** schools. Lewis loved going to church and wanted to be a preacher when he grew up. At home, his job was to take care of the chickens on the farm, and he remembers preaching to his chickens.

Much like Lewis's family, the sharecroppers pictured here in 1941 worked very hard for little return and poor living conditions.

OPEN EYES

John Lewis dealt with segregation much of his life. When he was a boy, it was considered normal that African American people lived in separate parts of town, rode at the back of the bus, went to different schools, and drank from separate water fountains. His eyes were opened when he took a trip with his uncle to Buffalo, New York.

Segregation was more **prominent** in the South. In northern cities, such as Buffalo, there was a little more equality. When they arrived at his uncle's house, Lewis couldn't believe that his uncle had white neighbors on both sides. In his book *March*, Lewis wrote, "After that trip, home never felt the same, and neither did I." He realized how different his life was from that of white children.

When Lewis was young, African American children couldn't attend the same schools as white children. The schools for African American children were supposed to be "separate, but equal," but that was never the case.

OFF TO COLLEGE

As a young man, Lewis loved books and school. He snuck away to class even when his father needed him on the farm. When he was a freshman in high school, the U.S. Supreme Court, in a case called *Brown v. Board of Education*, ruled that racial segregation in schools is **unconstitutional**. The next year, Lewis heard a preacher from Atlanta, Georgia, on the radio. The man's name was Martin Luther King Jr.

Lewis attended American Baptist Theological Seminary, an all-black college, to become a minister. However, he wanted to attend Troy University, which didn't allow black students. A civil rights lawyer asked to represent Lewis in a lawsuit against the state of Alabama for his admission to Troy. Unfortunately, Lewis's family said it was too dangerous to proceed with the lawsuit.

John Lewis and Coretta Scott King attended the unveiling of an engraving honoring Martin Luther King Jr. The engraving is on the steps of the Lincoln Memorial, where King gave his famous "I Have a Dream" speech.

MARTIN LUTHER KING JR.

Martin Luther King Jr. led the American civil rights movement from 1955 until his death in 1968. He fought for rights using nonviolent, peaceful methods. He served as president of the SCLC and organized many protests. His "I Have a Dream" speech is one of the most famous speeches in American history. King won the Nobel Peace Prize in 1964. Sadly, he was shot and killed in 1968.

SITTING STILL, MOVING FORWARD

Around 1958, Lewis began attending a black Baptist church in Nashville, Tennessee, where he met people who were organizing nonviolent protests. He started going to workshops organized by the Fellowship of Reconciliation. Lewis learned how to treat others with love and respect during protests.

One method of nonviolent protest is a sit-in. During sit-ins, people sit or stand somewhere they aren't supposed to be and refuse to move. Lewis and other civil rights **activists** started sitting at segregated lunch counters in stores in downtown Nashville. They were beaten and cursed at, but they sat still.

On February 27, 1960, Lewis was arrested for the first time for his involvement in a sit-in. The sit-ins continued. Months later, Nashville stores began serving food to black people at lunch counters.

John Lewis was arrested on April 29, 1964, for participating in a nonviolent protest in Nashville, Tennessee.

LEWIS AND THE
FREEDOM RIDERS

In March 1961, Lewis heard about a new mission from CORE. This group wanted to desegregate public transportation in the South. The U.S. Supreme Court had ruled in 1960, in *Boynton v. Virginia*, that segregation on buses and at bus and rail stations was unconstitutional. Still, many Southern states ignored the ruling. CORE tested this new ruling by sending African American and white volunteers called Freedom Riders on buses into the Deep South.

The Freedom Riders were often beaten and arrested. On Mother's Day 1961, a mob of angry white people attacked a bus carrying a group of Freedom Riders just outside Anniston, Alabama. The mob threw rocks, smashed windows, slashed tires, and threw a firebomb into the bus before beating riders with baseball bats.

ROSA PARKS

On December 1, 1955, a woman named Rosa Parks refused to give up her seat to a white man on a bus in Montgomery, Alabama. She was secretary of her local office of the NAACP. Parks was arrested for refusing to move. Her supporters started a **boycott** of the bus line that lasted 381 days. This led to a wave of civil rights protests across the United States.

This is a portrait of the Freedom Riders. John Lewis is in the front row, second from the right.

LEADER OF
NONVIOLENCE

In 1962, Lewis was elected to be a leader of the SNCC. The SNCC, often pronounced "snick," was founded in 1960 to support the lunch counter sit-ins. The committee wanted to spread a message of nonviolence to students and other people participating in protests. Its statement of purpose said: "Through nonviolence, courage displaces fear; love transforms hate."

Lewis had a lot of work to do. The summer and fall of 1962 were violent times in places across the South and Midwest. There were shootings and attacks in response to SNCC protests. Some people in the SNCC started questioning if they should be able to defend themselves and whether white people should be allowed to join. Lewis tried his best to bring peace to the committee amidst the **chaos**

As chairman of the SNCC, Lewis worked tirelessly to end segregation and create change in U.S. policy.

THE MARCH ON WASHINGTON

John Lewis was only 23 years old when Martin Luther King Jr. asked Lewis to join him in the March on Washington for Jobs and Freedom. This was a political rally in Washington, D.C., to raise awareness for the civil rights movement.

On August 28, 1963, more than 200,000 Americans, both black and white, gathered for the march. Lewis was one of the "Big Six" civil rights leaders present that day. Lewis spoke that day about supporting the civil rights bill, but only if it included certain things that helped African Americans reach equality. He asked the people of the crowd to remember that they were in the middle of a social **revolution** and to stand up for what they believed was right. He is the last speaker from the March on Washington still alive today.

Martin Luther King Jr. said the March on Washington was "the greatest demonstration of freedom in the history of the United States." The march ended with his "I Have a Dream" speech and the "Big Six" later met with President John F. Kennedy.

SETBACKS AND VICTORIES

As African Americans demanded equality, angry **white supremacists** fought back even harder. On September 15, 1963, members of the Ku Klux Klan (KKK), a white supremacist group, bombed the 16th Street Baptist Church in Birmingham, Alabama, during church services. Four young girls died and 21 people were hurt. This terrible event outraged America.

Despite major setbacks, the movement celebrated victory when President Lyndon B. Johnson signed the Civil Rights Act of 1964 into law on July 2, 1964. This law made racial segregation and discrimination illegal. Now Lewis and SNCC wanted to focus on black voter **registration**. Lewis had a very large role in helping African Americans in Mississippi exercise their constitutional rights. He coordinated voter registration drives and community action programs.

President John F. Kennedy was an advocate, or supporter, of the civil rights movement. When he was assassinated on November 22, 1963, Lewis was unsure of what would happen next.

MISSISSIPPI FREEDOM SUMMER

Segregation and discrimination were especially bad in Mississippi. There, SNCC campaigns were often unsuccessful because they were met with violence from segregationists. The Freedom Summer program in 1964 aimed to draw national attention to how African Americans in Mississippi were being treated and to create a freedom movement that would last even after the activists left Mississippi. More than 700 volunteers from across the United States helped register African American voters as part of the program.

A BLOODY
MARCH

Tensions had run high in Selma, Alabama, since 1963. White supremacists attacked a peaceful protest in February 1965, and a police officer shot a black man. This prompted Martin Luther King Jr. to plan a march from Selma to Montgomery, the capital of Alabama. Lewis would be on the front lines yet again, leading the marchers.

The first attempt to march from Selma to Montgomery happened on March 7, 1965. It became known as Bloody Sunday when Alabama police officers attacked protesters. Lewis's skull was broken and he almost died.

After this, President Lyndon B. Johnson gave his support and protection to the marchers. Starting on March 21, 1965, the marchers made it to Montgomery in four days. Later that year, on August 6, 1965, Congress passed the Voting Rights Act, which made racial discrimination in voting illegal.

Only two weeks after he was injured, Lewis marched with Martin Luther King Jr. and other civil rights leaders from Selma to Montgomery. Lewis is the farthest to the right.

HOUSE OF REPRESENTATIVES

In 1966, Lewis parted ways with the SNCC. However, that wasn't the end of his work for civil rights. He continued to work with voter registration programs, trying to give a voice to African Americans who had been silenced for too long. He became the director for the Voter Education Project, helping register close to four million **minorities**.

In 1981, Lewis was elected to serve on the city council in Atlanta, Georgia. Five years later, he became the U.S. representative of Georgia's Fifth Congressional District, a role that he's held for over 20 years. In 2011, President Barack Obama gave Lewis one of the highest honors in the country—the Presidential Medal of Freedom. Lewis has won many awards for his civil rights activism, leadership, and writings.

President Barack Obama presented Lewis with the Presidential Medal of Freedom on February 15, 2011.

PRESIDENT BARACK OBAMA

For many people, Barack Obama represents the great **diversity** in America. His father was from Kenya and his mother was a white woman from Kansas. He went to Harvard Law School and worked as a community organizer in Chicago. He became the first African American president of the United States in 2009 and was reelected in 2012. His message—"Yes we can!"—was one of hope for Americans everywhere.

GOOD TROUBLE

As a representative, John Lewis still has to fight for what he believes in. He is often outspoken about injustices and about political decisions that may harm Americans.

Lewis again entered the spotlight in 2016 when he led yet another sit-in. This one happened in the chamber of the House of Representatives. A mass shooting in Orlando, Florida, in June 2016 outraged Lewis and other Democratic representatives. They wanted tougher gun laws to prevent such shootings in the future.

Lewis and his fellow representatives sat shoulder to shoulder for hours, with more people joining in. He spoke to other lawmakers, saying, "Now is the time to get in the way. The time to act is now."

Lewis calls peaceful demonstrations, such as the sit-in in the House of Representatives to force a vote on gun control legislation, "good trouble."

HERO OF
CIVIL RIGHTS

John Lewis grew up in a time when a black man wasn't allowed to drink from the same water fountain as a white man. In 2009, he was able to see the first African American president of the United States—Barack Obama—sworn into office.

John Lewis fought for the American civil rights movement without a thought to the danger it brought him. He was beaten and jailed, and he looked death in the eye during marches and demonstrations. He kept his promise to be nonviolent even when he was faced with hateful people.

More than 50 years later, Lewis knows that there's still work to be done. As a U.S. representative, he's still willing to make "good trouble" to achieve equality and freedom

John Lewis marches with President Obama and his family in Selma, Alabama, to remember the struggles African Americans faced during the original march.

THE *MARCH* TRILOGY

John Lewis kept the spirit of the American civil rights movement alive when he wrote his memoir, *March*. The memoir is a series of graphic novels, or a story told through comics, that spans three books. The *March* books make the movement come alive for younger readers. The books tell the story of Lewis's childhood, the day he met Martin Luther King Jr., the fight of the Freedom Riders, and the marches in Washington, D.C., and Selma, Alabama.

TIMELINE

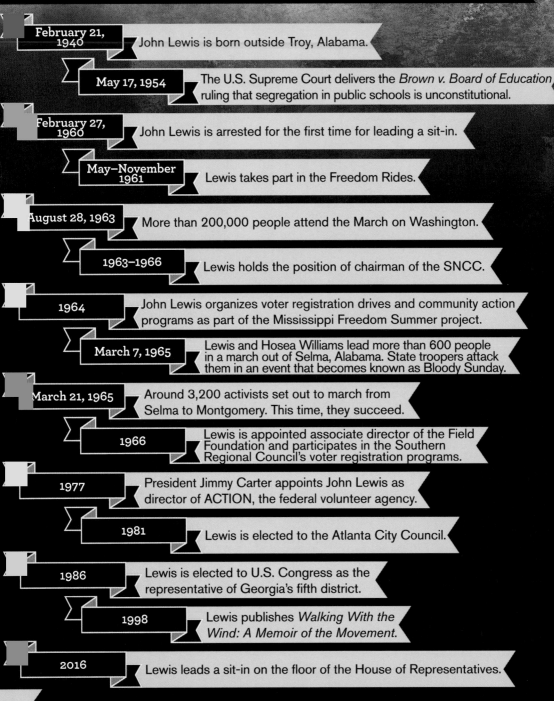

February 21, 1940 — John Lewis is born outside Troy, Alabama.

May 17, 1954 — The U.S. Supreme Court delivers the *Brown v. Board of Education* ruling that segregation in public schools is unconstitutional.

February 27, 1960 — John Lewis is arrested for the first time for leading a sit-in.

May–November 1961 — Lewis takes part in the Freedom Rides.

August 28, 1963 — More than 200,000 people attend the March on Washington.

1963–1966 — Lewis holds the position of chairman of the SNCC.

1964 — John Lewis organizes voter registration drives and community action programs as part of the Mississippi Freedom Summer project.

March 7, 1965 — Lewis and Hosea Williams lead more than 600 people in a march out of Selma, Alabama. State troopers attack them in an event that becomes known as Bloody Sunday.

March 21, 1965 — Around 3,200 activists set out to march from Selma to Montgomery. This time, they succeed.

1966 — Lewis is appointed associate director of the Field Foundation and participates in the Southern Regional Council's voter registration programs.

1977 — President Jimmy Carter appoints John Lewis as director of ACTION, the federal volunteer agency.

1981 — Lewis is elected to the Atlanta City Council.

1986 — Lewis is elected to U.S. Congress as the representative of Georgia's fifth district.

1998 — Lewis publishes *Walking With the Wind: A Memoir of the Movement*.

2016 — Lewis leads a sit-in on the floor of the House of Representatives.